The Cupid
Side of Me

The Cupid Side of Me

A Collection of Love Poems

Urbane Sleek

Library of Congress Control Number:		2019912271
ISBN:	Hardcover	978-1-7960-5414-9
	Softcover	978-1-7960-5413-2
	eBook	978-1-7960-5412-5

Print information available on the last page.

Rev. date: 08/22/2019

To order additional copies of this book, contact:
Xlibris
1-888-795-4274
www.Xlibris.com
Orders@Xlibris.com
800860

Contents

Adam & Eve 1

Baby Love 3

Bankruptcy of the Heart 5

Beauty & Attraction...7

Belizean Queen 9

Blinded 11

Crazy Skater 13

Cupids Flower 15

Cute Like Cartooned...17

Drawn...19

Earring 21

Falling In Love 23

Holding On To A Dream...25

Holiday Wife 27

How Pretty You Are To Me...29

Lost Platonics...31

Loves Quest 33

Memorable Moment...35

Mickey and Minnie...37

No Take Offs 39

Nostalgic Moment...41

Old Couples 43

Outer Space Chick 45

Pen, Paper, & Poem...47

Simpin'...49

Super Couples 51

The City 53

The Cupid Side of Us..55

Traditional Dating Fool 57

What He Like About Her 59

When She's Happy..61

When She's Mad...63

Thank you to all my family and friends love you all.

Dedicated to my brother Michael,
Miss you.

Adam & Eve

She arose at the break of dawn…
And now here she is traveling towards the falling Sun…
Night begins across the sky
And He…
God's sun…
Looks for She…
God's daughter…
Both birthed into the void like air from under water…
When She finds him
She finds out He lost a rib for her…
And would not just stick his neck out for her…
But even break his back to satisfy her…

Baby Love

I was still a baby when I first met my baby
We both were babies...
Didn't know much but I knew enough that...
When you became a lady
And I became a man
We would be mommy and daddy...
We wore our baby clothes to our first wedding...
The first time I ever wore a tuxedo...
You in your pink gown and ribbon around your hair
And us dancing like babies do...
You looked up to me...
And you followed my lead
Even though we were both babies...
You believed in the baby me
Like I believed in the baby you...
Innocent...
The purest bride and the purest groom...
Babies at our first wedding...
Before we could leap high enough
To jump the broom...

Bankruptcy of the Heart

Bankruptcy of the heart occurs because
The heart is rich with love…
But when you invest too much of it in someone
And you don't get a return on that investment;
It ends up broke…
That's why you must save
And carefully manage it.

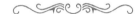

Beauty & Attraction

Beauty and attraction are in the volcano of the mind…
They erupt through smiles that crack on faces
And flow between beholders eyes.

Belizean Queen

Belizean Queen from the Caribbean's
Grown, sexy, and confident…
She oozes it…
I love it when a woman knows how to dress…
Knows how to impress…
And this lady is the beez-neezs
And Belize…
Please believe…
With feathers dangling from her ears
I asked her if that's what made her fly…
She replied…
"I'm fly on my own"…
See angel wings are grown
Not metal and feathers sown…
Her posture shows she's strong…
See…
You'd have to come right the first try
Because she don't do do-overs.
So if you mess up all you'll see is her back
And she don't look over her shoulders…
So it's you who turns to salt…
Trying to hold down something that belongs to the sky
To be visible for all earth surface admiring eyes…
Although she no longer resides in the city of Belize
I bet her hair still smells like the Caribbean Sea…
Probably mixed with a hint of Chicago breeze…
Too bad she moved to Minnesota…

I wish I knew her before she moved long distance;
Maybe we could have gone out
And ate some of her home town dishes...
Or...
Hit some Jamaican restaurant for some jerk chicken...

Blinded

Seen the woman of my dreams
And she told me to keep dreaming...
So I can't open my eyes because
Then I won't be seeing her...
So I walk around with my eyes closed...
Day dreaming...
Bumping into things that I say
Are just in the way.

Crazy Skater

I met her when she was resting
After skating from some other dude…
To him she got little before she disappeared
From his vision…
For me she became visible…
Appealable…
Available…
Single so I…
Glide pass her slowly
Then U-turn back
To ask for the seat next to her…
Still in her escape mode she tried to pretend she was crazy;
But when I made her smile
I saw that she was just a crazy skater…
An actor…
It's how she makes her way through the crowd of cards
That people get shuffled in…
So her mean face is just pretend…
She then lets me sit next to her
Both of us
Resting
From all the skating…
Not needing
To make a way through the crowd of card shuffling
Anymore
We're just side by side sitting out and chillin'…
While other skaters shuffle like cards around us

Cupids Flower

Surrounded by the sweet smell of summer
And a body of water,
Was a large patch of grass that lied magical flowers…
Planted by an angel
And with a seed of love,
A sparkle of his dust
Cupid made sure his flowers wouldn't bring forth lust…
His magical dust consisted of five important things
Loyalty, trust, honesty, comunication, and affection…
Each day cupid would tend to his flowers
To talk, to sing, and to nurture them…
In a matter of time his flowers grew
They were prettier than any star, rose, or jewel…
And when they blossomed,
Cupid gave one to every sincere man…
He told them that the flowers had one use only
So give it to the one they felt was worthy…
With that in mind the sincere men choose wisely
And their relationships haloed
On their fingers
And atop of their heads brightly…
They were ever after happy
And I am too…
Because I look forward to one day giving
My cupid flower to you…

Cute, Like Cartooned

She's like a cartoon
With the same kind of cute character…
Eyes that got me amazed in front of her in dream
Like a kid in front of a T.V screen…
She makes me feel just as innocent;

On good behavior because I love her show
Waking up earlier in the mornings just to look at her…
Her sexy illustration, eyes cute like cartooned;
What creator drew her eyes like that? Amazing
They're such beautiful animations…

She's my favorite show; she can actually
Look back at me…
She's realer than CG,
She's gorgeous, her smile has character
That's cute like cartooned…

And sometimes she's a comic;
A book of laughter and smiles that I can hold on to

Drawn

I drew you…
Penciled you in during my spare time…
Shaded you,
Recognize your dimensions
And married you on paper…
You give
The sheets value
And in your completion you're the art
Of the artist…
Forever you will remain this way;
Beautiful as the day I drew you..
And although our sheet will age
You'll always be what I imagined…
And I knew you would,
That's why I drew you
And penciled you in during my spare time…

Earring

I won't be an earring…
Because I like being
In your occipital lobe…
I'm not like those
Who've been in your dresser drawer;
I'm out of the box…
So if you want me
You'll have to look elsewhere to find me…

Falling In Love

And so they matrimony the space between them…
Freeing themselves of nots and instead twisting…
Foreheads touching…
Brains listening…
Hearts visiting each other's chest…
They've sunken into each other…
Fastened together basking in forever's moment…
Forever's sonnet…
"The World" quarreled round underneath them…
As they summited them…
Above as if summoned by Him…
All the while…
On earth…
In the cold bare feet upheave snow…
And in the rain toes wrinkle from being soaked…
While they levitated
Above the weathers
And float
Just to fall in love
And be caught by the clouds above…

Holding On To A Dream

The stage is small compared to the crowd
If they're rushing the stage in stadium…
And this was a thought
He had aloud to himself…
Holding a ball in an empty gymnasium…

Holiday Wife

I wonder what it would be like to have a wife during the holidays…
During the season's greetings and New Year preparations…
You seemed like a planner to me…
Someone who aesthetics
In decoratives
So…
You ornamenting a tree
Just came to me…
I don't know…
Seems like…
Christmas lights
Make holiday wives…
It's the way that they glow in them…
And amongst the silver bells ringing
Is the sound of the bracelets that you created on your wrist jingling…
Our stereo singing Christmas tunes
As we holiday on the other side of the broom
For the first time as a union…

How Pretty You Are To Me

Seeing your pretty face opens my eye's
A face in-which cries don't lie
Your pretty face it takes away pain
Launching thousands of ships in the rain. (Troy)

A beauty once lost a beauty now found
A beauty in-which a man has crowned
Beauty of beauties you'll always be
Cause you are just that pretty to me.

A pretty girl with a pretty smile
A girl with a pretty and sweet personile.
Filled with love not filled with hate
A girl with faith to this present date.

A beauty that's clear, a beauty that's near.
For you I promise I'll always be here.
Around the corner that's where I'll be
Waiting to tell you how pretty you are to me.

Lost Platonics

Could've played it different though…
Could've still had forever;
Could've still been an
'I love you friend'
With a kiss to the cheek
And or a hug at least;
Forever..
If ever..
I saw you again…

Loves Quest

To find a love Lord knows I've tried
A broken heart for each I've cried.
A heart un-mended no one intended
To love me in such a way I could feel it.

Searching for love in all the wrong places
All of this time good time has been wasted.
Searching so far searching so near
But so far I'm still the only one here.

Alone in my heart it feels so cold
No girl to love me… no girl to hold.
Maybe I'll find my soon to be
But for now I must leave all my heart breaks at sea.

Memorable Moment

As she lied on my chest singing…
Her vocal vibrations were recorded
By my main circulatory muscle…
And there it was saved as a memory
For me to recall anytime nostalgically…

Mickey and Minnie

She has a sweat voice
So I call her Minnie Mouse…
She even wears bows in her hair
And sometimes red dresses with white poker dots…
We smile and rub noses in our house of mouse…
Smiles we call cheese
That attract and trap one another as spouse…
I asked "would you be mines Minnie?"…
And she replied "I'm yours Mickey"…
Taking vacations
Walking hand in hand
Through the land
Of Walt Disney…
We're…
Drawn together as if made for each other…
Cute like cartooned…
Everyone's favorite...
Short lil' animated…
Couple…

No Take Offs

Why so cold?
Not lightly to impress or to amuse
To soothe…
My warmest mood couldn't thaw through you
And I'm pretty hot…
At least I think so…
To be alone…
Otherwise I'd be as cold as you
But perhaps you're metal
Cause even ice can melt ice if it's temper is different…
But the energy I give to you can't infuse…
For some reason there's never an ignition
It's getting to seem this ship might stall…
Due to lack of spark
No take offs…

Nostalgic Moment

Look to her as my baby
And she gives me her bottom lip…
At times we sit together in our Chaplin mutual…
No beautiful words…
Sweet nothings…
With the city in our window…

Old Couples

A lot of old couples use to be young couples…
Dressing like young adults for pictures
That their children's children
Will have them reminiscing on when asking them…
"How did they meet"…

Outer Space Chick

Talking to this chick from outer space…
A good distance away
So there's some delay in connection…
Wanted to see her in person
So I…
Jumped into my Urbane Sleek space ship
Just to get a closer look at her…
But the faster I went
The further away she became from me…
Thought she was accelerating away from me
But then I realized that it was the space
Between us that was expanding;
Causing us
To drift further apart in the vastness of space…
But still…
I try to keep contact with this outer space chick.
But the more space expands the harder it is to communicate…
The further away,
The longer the delay…
Can't catch up with her,
It's like she's light years away…
Never gave off light to my corner of space;
But still I can see her glowing…
Going…
Shifting to inferred as she moves further away
While those close to me see me as…
"Blue"…
Funny how time is over distances,
Especially in these instances

Where…
Now it takes weeks to hear from this outer space chick…
Feeling woes;
Because the voice messages I'm listening to are…
Months old…
Sometimes I catch myself staring off into space
Thinking about this outer space chick…
Only came in contact with
A Peace of her space ship…
Itself cloaked in War shade
Using the blanket of space to Masquerade…
Never seen her up-close
Only through pictures captured by lenses;
I wonder if they were taken by telescope…
Since I can't catch up with her
I guess I'll keep looking at her captured images
While she vanishes…
Perhaps in some
Champions arms…
Some
Selected selectee
Chosen by she…
Maybe it's together that they flee…
Disappearing in outer space
While I fall back to earth first by face…
But…
Still I often find myself starring off into space…
Thinking about this
Outer space chick…

Pen, Paper, & Poem

Skeet ink between mead sheets and birthed poem
A combination of me and her mom…
Can't look at her without seeing both of us…
Her mom's white background and my…
My imagination…
Since we became pen and paper you were in mind…
To make something so…
Creative,
So original,
So beautiful…
Grew from a baby stanza to a compositional work…
Admired by many but you were written for one in particular…
The hand that guided me knows who…
He pronounced me and your mom pen and paper
And will one day soon pronounce to you as Poem
To a reader…

Simpin'

Looking at her...
Reading her like the beautiful poetry that she is...
Her eye's read: seductively persuasive
Her lips read: enticingly kissable
All together she's the most sexiest and irresistible Queen
(Beauty mark) period...
Yeah she's definitely something serious...
Wish she was in front of me so I could...
Sketch over her countenance with my eyes
While daydreaming of tracing the curve of her left brow
With my bottom lip...
Leading into a temple kiss
Now that would be the shh...
Got me lost in my thoughts and caught in her gaze
Can't take my mind off her so I'm frequently in a daze...
Smiling for seemingly no reason out of the blue
Don't ask why I'm smiling you know It's cause of you...
She is...
The sonnet at the summit of my page
But...
Far away with other Kings looking her way...
And so...
On my page or hers is where I usually be
Trying to be unique in telling her how pretty she is to me...
And I'm sure she's heard it all before
But hopefully she won't mind hearing it just once more...
She probably got all the guys sipping on simp juice
Falling at her feet cutting their pimp loose...
Looking for shackles to fasten at their feet

Trying to ball and chain hers' cause their playing for keeps...
And here I am 26 and probably out of my league
But does that mean I shouldn't attempt to try to get her intrigued?
Or try to get her with me?
Or flirt with her through poetry?
Hoping that she can see the potential in me
To potentially be
Someone who she can think of intimately
Who stimulates her mentally...
Yeah I'm trying to be all up in her mind like she's in mine
Trying to move at her pace taking it one step at a time...
Don't know if she likes me but then again it doesn't really matter
Because I still think she's a beautiful person and I enjoy our chit chatter...
Love how she inspires and makes me smile
Giving me feelings I haven't had in a while...
She's a wonderful friend....
Couldn't ask for one better
Try to restrain from calling cause I don't want to sweat her...
But just know...
Queen...
You are appreciated...
From your beautiful sculpture to your inner poem
The art about you is what keeps me showing
Up on your page to leave a flirt...
If you're reading this poem and think it's not about you
It's probably because I wrote it for....... Who?

Super Couples

Superwomen fly solo like Supermen do
Unless someone can keep up…
If you can't…
Maybe they'll Hero and hold you up
But if not…
Then in their escape
All you'll see is their cape
And all you'll have is a story
About the one time
That you were saved…

The City

Walking…
Heads held high looking up toward the sun
Just to have a warm smile to share with one another…
Summer days would be their everyday;

But sometimes the city conjures up winds that run pass
Smiling faces;
Turning them into cold quivering lips…

Heads drop and bodies shiver
Trying to find comfort through those coldest temperatures;
Those coldest times...
Where even when the sun is out, it's hard to see it shine…

To busy bundling up instead of opening up,
Stuck inside of their shell slash winters coat…
Watching their steps as they walk down icy roads;
Keeping to themselves because their words could get cold…

Eye's squinted as if suspicious of one another;
But really it's the cold winds making them teary eyed…
Squinting keeps their tears from freezing,
By attempting to keep them held on the inside…

Waiting…

For those days when the city emits light that soothes quiverig lips;
Turning them into warm beautiful smiles...
Heads rise to bathe their faces in the sun,
Just to have a warm smile to share with one another...

The Cupid Side of Us

While kids lie in the snow trying to make angels
Me and you lie in the clouds trying to make kids…
And we giggle just like them…
That's the cupid side of us
We look and seem like children in puppy love
With one another…
Playing with each other and tickling
Sitting close to one another; cuddling…
The cupid side of you, in love with the cupid side of me.
We connect with each other's grown youthful selves…
No one else
Can bring out our cupid side;
Our cutest smiles,
Our innocent eyes…
No room for other archers on our cloud
We already have each other's arrows in our hearts…
So no other arrows will make their mark,
For our cloud is our heaven, it's why our halos spark…
Our matching rings and wings,
Our God's entrusting…
These are encompassing
And these are what make up
What we both know as the cupid side of us…

Traditional Dating Fool

I knew something was wrong with her
Even though she wouldn't admit it…
She just quietly ate her ice cream
As if we were not on a date…
I wondered who or what she had her mind on
But she wouldn't let me look into her eyes
So I couldn't read her mind…
I could feel the heartbreak coming…
Using my fork to play with my food because…
Now I didn't feel like eating…
I'd rather be let down on an empty stomach
That way I could fast from her…
Get her out of my system…
Kind of upset though because
I got dressed up and paid for this break up…
I'll leave hungry and hurt
While she leaves
Relieved and full…
Happy because she's now free to do
What she really wants to…
Making me a traditional dating fool…

What He Like About Her

I see what he like about her..
She's extremely elegant,
Delicate and refined…
Spiritually a
Heavenly celestial beauty
From the upper regions…
Above E.T's
She's…
Probably out of his league…
Imperial, ethereal, and spiritual
With sunrise in her sclera's…
A dream, a flower, an arrow..

When She's Happy

And when she's happy…
I vision her dancing atop of furniture meant for sitting next to.
I vision myself watching from reaching distance
Undulating my head to the same rhythm of her sway
Trying to keep in tune as she music surfs

When She's Mad

"Oh Lady"...
Is what I say with a smile on my face
Because she's mad at me...
And she's so cute when she shows it...
I just want to apologize to her...
Kiss her whole face until she blushes cause...
I need to make up with her...
Can't be sleeping and eating in another room
Without her spoon...
Without her back against my chest
With our hearts lined up next to each other's...
Looking at the back of her head in bed
Talking to grace and saying thanks
With my arm around my lady...
Happy...
Making sure she knows that I love her
Even when she's mad

CPSIA information can be obtained
at www.ICGtesting.com
Printed in the USA
BVHW031017060919
557777BV00006B/62/P